TEDDY BEARS
in
Advertising Art

by Marty Crisp

Published by Hobby House Press

Hobby House Press, Inc.
Cumberland, Maryland 21502

Dedication
For Ma & Dad, who help me organize and MB, Bud, Will,
and Josh who plunge me back into happy confusion.

Additional copies of this book may be purchased at $12.95
from
Hobby House Press
900 Frederick Street
Cumberland, Maryland 21502
or from your favorite bookstore or dealer.
Please add $4.75 per copy for postage.

*On the cover: The bear is a cut-
out from an advertisement for
Roblee Shoes for Men, from
Life magazine, September 28,
1942. The teddy bear is a Dixie
cup cut-out, circa 1939.*

Printed in the United States of America
ISBN: 0-87588-377-X

Table of Contents

Teddy Bears in Advertising Art
A Collector's Guide to Bears in Advertising

WANTED: A spokesperson who is warm, friendly, loved by the general public, and works "cheap."

Where could any company find such a wonder?

As close as the nearest teddy bear! The hardworking, tireless stuffed bear has been used as a symbol for everything from dry cereal to automotive repair. Since teddy bears never lie, businesses that use a bear as their trademark or as a related promotion can be seen as trustworthy, dependable, and concerned about the customer.

It is this impeccable reputation that has made the teddy bear so popular in advertising. And not just the teddy bear, either. All kinds of bears have been used in advertising over the past century, identifying products with the real animal's strong, silent reputation; fierce without being mean and almost human with humorous curiosity and playfulness.

Research in the field of advertising bears reveals that they are frequently used in advertisements for airlines, appliances, banks, beer, candy, cereal, charities, child care, cleaning compounds, hotels, ice cream, juice, liquor, soap, soda, snack food, sports teams, states or recreational areas, toy stores, vegetables, wine and zoos.

Covering the A-to-Z of bears in advertising, the furry creatures have been spotted on occasion in places you would never expect to find them, as salesmen for: aluminum products, batteries, blankets, blue jeans, cameras and film, cheese, cigars, computers, corsets, diapers, disinfectant, furs, gloves, hair care products, medicine, motor oil, pianos, railroads, records, restaurants, sandpaper, shoe polish, sports clothes, tailors, thread, tools, toothpaste, underwear, vacuum cleaners, varnish and video stores.

Bears are popular in advertising all over the world. In general, polar bears represent coolness and freshness or cleanliness and whiteness. Grizzlies and black bears represent strength. Cubs represent playfulness. And stuffed teddies represent gentleness and safety.

In recent years, it has been a bull market (gaining in value) for not only the manufacture and sale of bears, but also for the use of bears in every conceivable type of advertising. Whereas prices of old teddy bears have skyrocketed far past the reach of many bargain-hunting collectors, advertising bears, both on paper and in 3-D, remain affordable. Frequently, new advertisement bears are free.

Yet because promotional items are often only available for a limited time, their value is sometimes comparable to current high-priced limited edition bears. Unlike those limited editions, prices start low, but, like their pricier ursine brothers, they quickly escalate. Early Kellogg's cut-and-stuff Three Bears sets, available as a free promotional in 1926, easily bring over $500 today. Clairol Before-And-After Bears, from the 1950s, cost less than $10 for a set when first offered to beauty parlors but now would bring $300 or more.

Print advertisements for the 1900s through the 1960s, free to anyone who cut them out and saved them when they were first published in magazines and newspapers, now sell for $5 to $25 each.

Advertising bears are a hot new collectible, with high crossover appeal to the many collectors of advertising ephemera. Companies with no relation to teddy bears more and more frequently feature stuffed actors in the photo portions of their advertisements, looking for that undeniable good feeling associated with the teddy. Bears are stars almost everywhere in the advertisement firmament.

In fact, there is only one area of advertising and promotion where bears are not used to inspire confidence and comfort. On Wall Street the bear has long been dreaded as a symbol of gloom, representing a market where prices of investments are falling and people are losing money.

Cartoon from the December 1929 Chicago Tribune — *the rivalry of bulls and bears was used as imagery to comment on events in the stock market.*

A Bull Market for Bears

How did the otherwise sterling reputation of the bear suffer this slight to his name?

Just as there are several conflicting stories about how the teddy bear got its name, there are different theories on why Wall Street named a falling market after the bear.

Bears and Bulls are the popular names for two particular points-of-view among those who invest in stocks and commodities.

Some believe the expressions come from the differing way the two animals attack their enemies. A bear attacks by sweeping its paws downward. A bull attacks by tossing its horns up in the air.

One 19th century observer noted that, if a bear finds "a turkey on the roost or a man in a tree, he lifts his paw and pulls it down. The bull, on the contrary, lowers his head only to give men and things a decided upward tendency."[1]

A bearish investor expects prices to fall and sells with the hope of being able to buy back at a cheaper price later. A bear may also be an investor who has sold short, that is, sold a commodity or a security before having actual or complete possession of it. A bear market, therefore, comes when more people want to sell than buy, and prices fall.

A bullish investor believes prices will go up and buys in anticipation of a market advance. When more people want to buy than sell, prices rise and we have a bull market.[2]

Some say the use of the terms "bulls" and "bears" originated in England in the early 18th century, based on the old proverb, "Don't sell the bearskin before the bear is caught."[3] Traders who sold short, expecting prices to fall, became known as "bear skin jobbers." The origin

5

"The Battle of the Bulls and the Bears" from Harper's Weekly, *September 10, 1864.*

THE BATTLE OF THE BULLS AND BEARS.

"Humpty Dumpty on a wall,
Humpty Dumpty got a fall?"

of "bull" is not known in this version of the phrase, except that the word bull was often associated with bears.

During the 18th century, both bull-baiting and bearbaiting were popular sports, in which a tethered animal was attacked by a pack of dogs. The phrase caught on as a general description of the frenzied atmosphere of stock trading.[4]

The first recorded use of "bulls and bears" was in 1721 by British playwright Colley Cibbler in his play "Refusal" (Act I).

"And all this out of Change Alley? (the London Stock Exchange)

"Every shilling, Sir; all out of stocks, tuts, bulls, rams, bears, and bubbles."[5]

Probably the earliest reference in the United States, although the terms were considered slang at the time, was in a June 4, 1884, article in the *Chicago Times*: "If we succeed in bulling silver, we shall also succeed in bearing gold to the same extent."[5]

Another theory on the origin of the phrase is that, since a market bear seeks to depress prices, the name comes from the verb "to bear," meaning "to press heavily upon." Still another camp says that "bear" comes from "bare." Because a bear investor has sold short stocks he does not own, he is "bare of stocks."[2]

Bull may have come from the farm reference to bulls lifting things with their horns, just as market bulls lift up prices.

Market bears are unpopular, and are considered unpatriotic, because they seem to bet against a country's well-being. They profit from falling prices that are bad for the rest of the population. Wealthy financier J.P. Morgan once said, "Remember, my son, that any man who is a bear on the future of this country will go broke."[5]

The one consolation for bear lovers is the commonly held belief among Wall Streeters that a bull market begins when things are darkest, but a bear market begins when everything is bright and going well.

Of course, the symbolic Wall Street Bear is not a popular animal in the skyscraper canyons of southeast Manhattan, since he represents a down-swing in market prices.

On the other hand, it is ironically a bear market for bulls. Except for their status as representatives of an upswing in market prices, bulls are little used in advertising and seldom found as stuffed toys.

So what if the beloved bear plays the bad guy in the Wall Street scenario? A villain's role is considered a challenge by any leading actor, a way to expand his repertoire and hone his skills.

References:
[1] *World Book Encyclopedia*, 1986.
[2] *New York Stock Exchange, Inc.*
[3] *A Hog On Ice and Other Curious Expressions*, Charles Funk, 1948.
[4] *High Steppers, Fallen Angels, and Lollipops*, 1988, Kathleen Odean.
[5] *Oxford English Dictionary*, 1933.

Opposite Page: Cover of the May 18, 1901 Harper's Weekly.

Vol XLV   No 2317   10 Cents a Copy

HARPER'S
WEEKLY

A JOURNAL OF   CIVILIZATION

NEW YORK   MAY 18, 1901

THOSE LAMBS WERE GETTING TOO "CHESTY"

"Bears and Bulls of the Market" by William Holbrook Beard.

The Stockbearoker *from North American Bear Co.*

A bull that turns into a bear from Gadzooks.

Bookends.

Cartoon from the December 1929 Chicago Tribune.

Bull & Bear slippers comfort the modern investor. Photograph of Josh Crisp.

TAME THE MARKET
WITH COMPUSERVE

The Bear Boom

It is a bull market for bears.

If teddy bear stock were being traded on the floor of the New York Stock Exchange today, a buying frenzy would certainly occur.

Advertisers worldwide have wisely made the bear a star when it comes to salesmanship. The display windows of a medical supply store in my town feature a five foot stuffed teddy pushing a wheelchair, with smaller bears clinging to canes and sitting on adult potty seats.

It is the "spoonful-of-sugar-makes-the-medicine-go-down" theory at work. Teddy bears even make crippling disabilities seem less threatening. The comfort of a hug is something every teddy promises...and unfailingly delivers.

Fehr's beer plaster of paris bar display.

A whiskey decanter.

A paper bear advertisement for Barney's sandpaper.

Bear on Paper

Behr Manning was located in Troy, New York, and manufactured by Norton Abrasives. Its triangular trademark enclosed a line drawing of a standing bear. That bear was transformed into the promotional "Barney Bear." Used as a paper bear in the 1930s, Barney is a brown bear standing on a mound of green grass.

His appearance changed slightly in the course of the paper bear promotional series, but the costumes provided for him always had one thing in common: they were occupation-oriented, Barney dressed up as everything from a fireman to a sailor to an Indian Chief.

19

A Leg Up

Bear Brand Hosiery, manufactured in both Illinois and Wisconsin, was made for both men and women. The blurb from an advertising leaflet found inside a Bear Brand box reads: "The spinning of cotton and throwing of silk under our supervision insures for the consumer a uniform product of the greatest possible value."

Bear Brand offered a premium bear in the 1920s. "Benny Bear" was advertised as 11in (28cm) high and ready to be sewn and stuffed. He cost 10 cents.

Bear Brand Hosiery advertisement.

The jingle attached to his advertisement campaign was:"
My name is Benny,
I'm a little cloth bear.
I'll come to your house,
If you'll just pay my fare."

Bear Brand Hosiery

An early manufacturer of silk and nylon stockings, Bear Brand Hosiery featured a bear on the box and came out with several premiums in the early 1900s, including a paper bear with movable legs. The only known stuffed version of the Bear Brand Hosiery bear was actually a variation of the ever-popular Three Bears. Three flat cloth dolls, circa late 1920s, each 9in (23cm) high and each holding a box of Bear Brand Hosiery were printed in bright colors on heavy muslin for cut-and-sew fun at home. Papa Bear wears a jacket, tie, and checkerboard pants; Mama Bear wears a blue skirt with yellow dots and a white blouse with a red bow at the neck; and Baby Bear wears blue jeans and a red t-shirt with one yellow stripe. These bears are rare, especially in good condition, and the value of a complete set would be approximately $500.

Bear Brand Hosiery promotional item.

"The Three Bears" booklet, a promotional item given away with Ma-le-na salve.

Golden Bears Cookies tin of 1930s vintage.

Polar Ginger Ale serving tray.

A box of Bear Cleaner and Water Softener.

Kellogg's Johnny Bear promotional item.

Pettijohn's Breakfast Food advertisement.

Household Bears

Pettijohn's Breakfast Food was manufactured in California in the 1890s and early 1900s. The bear symbol used by the company probably derives from the California state symbol of a bear.

As active rival of Quaker Oats, Pettijohn's slogan was: "I eat wheat — my horse eats oats."

Made in Chicago, Illinois, the now defunct company offered such promotionals as "Mother Goose in Prose" by L. Frank Baum (author of *The Wizard of Oz*), available for three bear symbols cut from the package and eight cents in stamps. This offer was made in June 1900, when the company also claimed that nurses recommended their cereal and that it was a delicious substitute for meat. At this point, the bears in the ad-

vertisements looked very bearish, as did the bear in the trademark symbol.

By 1902, the bears looked more teddyish, and always included two mischievous cubs, sometimes with and sometimes without their patient Mama Bear. Pettijohn's, part of the larger American Cereal Company, made a number of humorous and sometimes amazing claims in its advertisements, including: "Breakfast must be appetizing — no one is hungry for breakfast" and "Pettijohn's does not weaken your stomach for the want of something to do. It puts red into your blood."

The Pettijohn bear cubs, likewise, put warmth and humor into their product's advertising campaign.

Bears Beloved by Beers

It is not clear why bears and beer seem to go together so well (and so often). However, a bear has been used as the symbol for Hamm's Beer, Grizzly Beer, White Bear Beer, Polar Beer, Big Bear Ale, and Fehr Beer.

White Bear Beer was made by the White Bear Brewing Company of Thorton, Illinois, from 1949 to 1955. This company was an offshoot of the Walter Brewing Company of Euclair, Wisconsin, which reused the White Bear gimmick from 1965 to 1969 and again from 1974 to the present. White Bear cans are aimed at breweriana collectors, and replica cans abound. Original cans from the 1949 to 1955 period are very rare and cost as much as $300.

Polar Beer, made in Mexico in the 1960s and 1970s also used a white polar bear as its symbol.

Big Bear Ale was made by Eastern Brewing Company, Hammonton, New Jersey, from 1946 to 1950. This was the time period when there were still some 6000 breweries, many small, hometown operations, in production. Today, there are about 20 major breweries in the United States.

Fehr Beer Bear used a teddy bearish white bear as the symbol for its product, made in Louisville, Kentucky, from 1874 to 1964. The beer, also manufactured in Louisiana and Ohio, was based at a location on 412-430 Fehr (pronounced "fur") Avenue in Louisville, and was first made by Brohm and Fehr (1874 to 1875) and later by Frank Fehr Brewery (1876 to 1964). Although trays and cap knobs imprinted with the bear's image are still available, a heavy plaster bar display, showing the cub holding a bottle in one

Polar Beer bear advertisement.

White Bear beer advertisement.

paw and an ice pick in the other, is the only figural ever made of this rare and charming advertising symbol. Value: $250.

The Hamm's Beer Bear, Pabst Brewing Company, has been featured in radio, television, and print advertisements for over 20 years. The beer itself was first

Grizzly Beer bottle label.

brewed in 1865, and its slogan is "American's Classic Premium Beer — Brewed in the land of sky blue waters." The Hamm's Beer coaster is marked "Theo. Hamm Brewing Co., St. Paul, Minn. — San Francisco, Calif."

Grizzly Bear Beer is a Canadian lager, first brewed in the early 1980s. Other beer bears probably exist or did exist somewhere. It is a popular combination.

White Bear Beer was made during the 1950s, by the Walter Brewing Company of Eau Claire, Wisconsin. Some cans were marked "Strong" because of a higher-than-usual alcohol content of the beer. The replica can in the photograph cost $1.00. An original can of this brand is extremely rare and can bring up to $300. The Grizzly Beer bar display is a molded, lightweight plastic bear and base. The beer is a Canadian lager, brewed and bottled by Hamilton Breweries, Hamilton and Ontario, Canada. It comes in a green glass 12 ounce bottle, labeled "imported," and a friendly-looking grizzly bear is featured in the product's logo. First available in the United States in 1984, this is a new item in the breweriana market, and sells for about $30.

Grizzly Beer promotional item.

Guinness ale advertisement, September 1945.

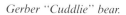

Gerber "Cuddlie" bear.

Getty Oil bear.

All bears this page courtesy of Millie Natale
Collection.

The Shoprite bear.

Ice Capades "Ice Follies" bear.

27

Hamm's beer bar display.   *Sleepytime Bear from Celestial Seasonings.*

A Household Bear
with no Caffeine

One advertising teddy definitely designed to help his owners sleep at night is Celestial Seasonings Sleepytime Bear. This 1985 promotional is a limited edition of 10,000 and cost under $20 (plus a box top, of course!). He is manufactured by Trudy Toys of Norwalk, Connecticut, and wears an attached red flannel nightcap and a removable white flannel nightshirt.

The tea he promotes, from Celestial Seasonings, Inc., Boulder, Colorado, is a blend of chamomile, spearmint, passion flower, lemon grass, blackberry leaves, orange blossoms, hawthorn berries, skullcap and rosebuds. It is billed as "a soothing tea for a nervous world," and the box pictures the Sleepytime Bear dozing in his easy chair by the fireplace,

while Mama Bear leads the two bear cubs off to bed.

The huggable 16in (41cm) brown plush bear seems to fit in well with the company's philosophical approach to life and salesmanship. The bottom of the 24-bag tea box quotes this delightful limerick by Anthony Euwer:

"No matter how grouchy you're feeling,

You'll find the smile more or less healing

It grows in a wreath

All around the front teeth,

Thus preserving the face from congealing."

Certainly, no bear could ask for more than to bring a smile to a person's face.

Teddy Snow Crop

Teddy Snow Crop is the symbol for Snow Crop Orange Juice, a division of the Coca Cola Company, Inc. The first bear offered as a promotional from this company was in the early 1950s — an 8½ in (22cm) plush hand puppet with a gray vinyl face. A 10in (25cm) white plush stuffed bear with vinyl mask face was also offered around 1955 to 1957. This hard-to-find item has a value of $50.

Super Sugar Crisp Bear.

Bear in a Bottle

Snuggle, the fabric softener bear from Lever Brothers, is a 1982 addition to the premium bear market. He appears in television commercials as a white, curly plush teddy, with a soft childlike voice and huggable look. He was created for Lever Brothers by Kermit Love, the white-haired, white-bearded genius who created Big Bird for Sesame Street. Snuggle is a registered trademark for the new Lever Bros. laundry product, featured on calendars, and in a 6in (15cm) stuffed version by Russ, with a cloth tag marked "Snuggle."

Snuggles, the Snuggle Fabric Softener bear.

Chicago cubs ceramic nodder from about 1985.

L'eggs teddy bear, courtesy Millie Natale Collection.

American Lung Association bear, courtesy Millie Natale Collection.

Crocker Bank bear premium.

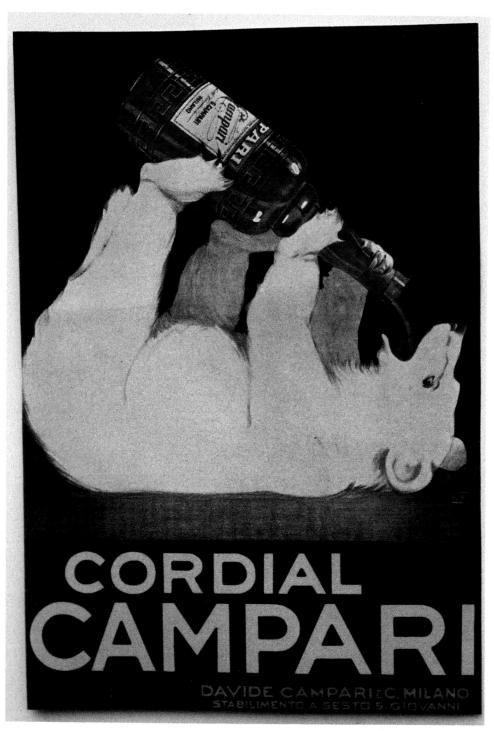

Cordial Campari Poster by F. Laskoff 1938 Davide Campari & Co.

Giorgio perfume bear.

Godiva Chocolates bear.

Big A Auto Parts bear.

All bears this page, courtesy of
Millie Natale Collection.

Fiddle Faddle popcorn bear.

Berlin bear.

National Video "Viddy-O" bear.

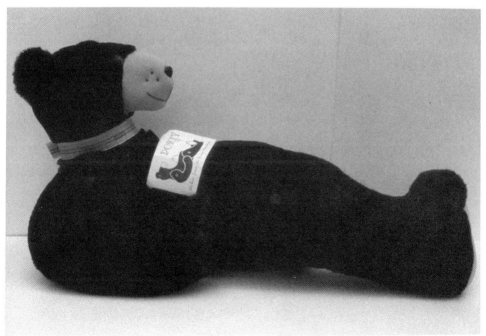

Poconos' resorts "Pokey."

Fuji Film koala bear, Millie Natale Collection.

Tru Hardware TruValue bear, Millie Natale Collection.

Dairy Queen "Strawbeary Bear."

Peter Panda of Children's Palace toy stores.

Great Bear Natural Spring Water bottle with label.

Great Bear Natural Spring Water label.

Dole "Bananabear."

Bear broccoli label.

Kellogg's Yogi Bear and Huckleberry Hound advertisement.

Rumple-Minze liquor advertisement.

Child's Tommee Tippee drinking cup.

Klondike ice cream bars.

Aunt Jemima premium offer from 1988.

Girl Scout Cookies advertisement, Millie Natale Collection.

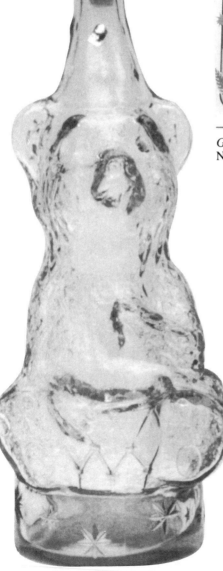

Bear-shaped wine decanter, Millie Natale Collection.

The Clairol "Before" bear is crying because she is unhappy about her looks. The 15in (38cm) brown plush bear has molded face with straight, scraggly-looking bangs and a blue ribbon around her neck.

The Clairol "After" bear is happy because she has a forehead full of tight honey-blonde curls. She has a red ribbon around her neck. Both bears were offered in 1958 to hairdressers to display with their Clairol items. Due to their limited availability then, they are very hard to find currently. Both bears have cloth tags that read "The Rushton Co., Atlanta, Ga." Both are paper straw stuffed and have stub tails. They are valued at over $500 for both in mint condition.

Imperial whiskey advertisement from 1943.

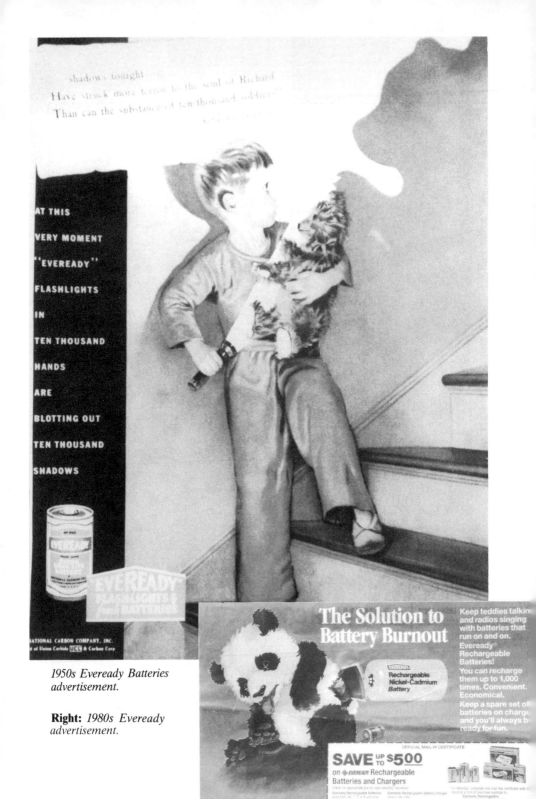

1950s Eveready Batteries advertisement.

Right: *1980s Eveready advertisement.*

"Fuzzie, Wuzzie and the Bee Tree," a 1914 premium offered with Little Bo-Peep ammonia. Number 10 in a series.

"Fuzzie, Wuzzie and the Playhouse," a 1914 premium offered with Little Bo-Peep ammonia. Number 12 in a series.

Kodak Kodacolor advertisement from 1989.

A Kodak Story

of the baby—a serial story from the Teddy bear days, through childhood and school days until home ties are broken—such a story has the charm of human interest, the interest that endures.

And it's an easy story to record, for the Kodak works at the bidding of the merest novice. There is no dark-room for any part of Kodak work, it's all simple. Press the button—do the rest—or leave it to another—just as you please.

Catalogue free at the dealers or by mail.

EASTMAN KODAK CO.

Rochester, N.Y., *The Kodak City.*

Piper Cub advertisement from Life *magazine, May 8, 1943.*

Piper Cub advertisement from Life *magazine, October 11, 1943.*

Buchan's soap offered six postcards for the return of one wrapper in 1907.

Pettijohn's Breakfast Food advertisements from 1899 to 1902. Note how the bear becomes very teddy-like in the circa 1902 advertisement at the bottom left. The bottom right advertisement is an offer for "Mother Goose in Prose Free" for three bears cut from Pettijohn's Breakfast Food packages and eight cents in stamps to pay for mailing.

Pettijohn's Breakfast Food
THE WHOLE OF THE WHEAT

Nurses Recommend It.

The happiness which springs from perfect health is alone ample reason why you should eat little meat in summer, and **Pettijohn's Breakfast Food**, which contains all the elements of nutrition, affords an easy, perfectly satisfactory and delicious substitute for meat. All of the wheat but the overcoat.

At all Grocers,
In 2-lb. Packages.

Pettijohn's Breakfast Food
ALL THE WHEAT BUT THE OVERCOAT

That satisfied—well-fed feeling.

There's a satisfied—well-fed feeling after a breakfast of delicious Pettijohn's. It satisfies that natural craving for wholesome food. Pettijohn's is a rich full-flaked wheat food, not an illogical granular or powdered wheat that cooks into a tasteless, starchy mass. Pettijohn's is full-flaked. It never deceives.

Besides being so easily and quickly prepared breakfast dish, delicious appetizing and nourishing. Pettijohn's Breakfast Food makes superb dish of Griddle Cakes, Gems, Muffins and Puddings. Ask us when ordering for Soups. Cold Pettijohn's Pottridge in the summer. Write for our Cereal Cook Book, edited by Mrs. Rorer. It tells all about cooking all kinds of cereals, all sorts of ways. Sent free, postpaid.
THE AMERICAN CEREAL CO. Monadnock Bldg., Chicago, Ill.

A WARM, FRESHLY-COOKED BREAKFAST
of
Pettijohn's Flaked Breakfast Food

assures outdoor, as well as indoor, health in winter.

It is an easily digested food, *not* pre-digested. Pettijohn's does not weaken your stomach for the want of something to do. It puts red into your blood—vitalizes it—makes you feel alive and vigorous through and through.

No food gives such flavor, such strength, health and lasting benefit as freshly-cooked food. Pound for pound Pettijohn's costs only half as much as ready cooked cereals,—and for the money spent gives four times the amount of nutriment.

MOTHER GOOSE IN PROSE FREE

Pettijohn's Breakfast Food
ALL THE WHEAT BUT THE OVERCOAT

FREE   MOTHER GOOSE IN PROSE.   **FREE**

By FRANK BAUM
Beautifully printed and illustrated. In 12 parts.
"It not only pleases children, but laughter is awakened by it in founded."—*Boston Transcript.*
"A set of artistic stories to from the little ones."—*Chicago Evening Post.*
"It is sure to keep the children happy."—*St. Louis Post Dispatch.*
To secure cut three Bears cut from Pettijohn's Breakfast Food package and 8 cents in stamps to pay for mailing, and we will send you FREE a copy of the first part of **Mother Goose in Prose.**
THE AMERICAN CEREAL CO.,   Monadnock Bldg., Chicago, Ill.

Avoid mushy, starchy, pasty breakfast cereals by eating Pettijohn's Breakfast Food. Each flake of Pettijohn's Breakfast Food is a thin, delicate wafer containing all of the nutrition of one large plump kernel of choicest Pacific Coast wheat. Unlike granulated cereals it may be properly cooked without becoming a starchy, unpalatable mush.

A Way to Start the Day

The first dry cereal was produced as a health food for patients at the Seventh-Day Adventist Sanitarium in Battle Creek, Michigan. In the 1880s, Dr. John H. Kellogg, Chief of Staff at the sanitarium, decided to go into business, selling the granola-type product he had invented. He started the Sanitos Food Company.

William Keith Kellogg, John's younger brother, managed the fledgling company and built it into a successful mail-order food enterprise. Quite by accident, while experimenting with a batch of cooked wheat one night, William invented the corn flake. The product was patented May 31, 1894.

An ambitious and inventive advertiser, William began offering advertising premiums in 1925. It was also at this time that the cereal's name was changed from Sanitos Corn Flakes to Kellogg's Corn Flakes. The Kellogg Company has offered over 90 doll premiums over the years, the very first being Goldilocks and The Three Bears in 1925. This first issue ranges in height from 12in to 15in (31cm to 38cm) and came printed on flat material in six lithographed colors. It cost 10 cents plus one box top for one figure, or 30 cents plus four box tops for the complete set of four. This premium was reissued in 1926 in a slightly different version.

Mama Bear.

Daddy Bear.

Johnny Bear.

In the 1925 issue, Goldilocks, 14in (36cm) tall, appears frightened and wears a lace trimmed dress and apron. "Kellogg's" is printed on the apron.

Papa Bear, 15in (38cm) tall, wears green pants with blue window pane checks, has a red jacket with yellow cuffs and holds a box of Kellogg's cereal in his paws. Mama Bear, 14in (36cm) tall, holds a bowl of cereal marked Kellogg's. She wears a red skirt, yellow blouse and dust cap. Baby or "Johnny" Bear, 12in (31cm) tall, wears polka-dot pants and also holds a bowl of Kellogg's cereal.

In the 1926 issue, Goldilocks wears a white skirt with red, green and blue flowers decorating it, and the word "Kellogg's" imprinted on the front waist. Daddy Bear, 13in (33cm) tall, wears a blue jacket with green trim, and yellow-and-red striped pants. Mama Bear, 13in (33cm) tall, wears a dainty lace edged apron over her blue striped dress, and Johnny Bear, 10in (25cm) tall, wears blue-and-white striped pants and a red shirt. This issue has the name of each character stamped on the reverse side.

Kellogg's definitely started something with its premium design. During the 1930s, it became common to see imprints stamped on the cloth sacks packaging sugar. Once cut out, stitched, and stuffed with cotton, they became economical rag dolls and stuffed animals at a bargain price.

Copy from the 1953 Texaco anti-freeze advertisement with a panda-like bear reads "Texaco Dealers in all 48 states."

1939 Texaco advertisement also has bears climbing the Texaco logo.

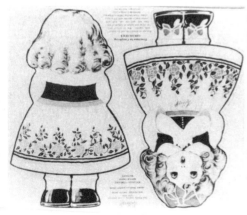

Goldilocks.

Bear Baker

The former Teddy Bear Bread Company, based in Detroit, Michigan, advertised its product with the slogan: "Every bite a delight." A turn-of-the-century bakery, Teddy Bear Bread used large (30in [76cm]), fully-jointed mohair bears in the windows of its bakeries as one of the earliest American advertising promotionals.

Like the Clairol Bears of the 1950s, these bears were generally available to dealers only (in this case bakeries) and not to the public. One such bear, acquired in 1904, and discovered by the Michauds of Carousel Museum in Michigan, cost $25 at time of purchase. It was purchased right out of a bakery window by a doting grandmother for her granddaughters. Although other Teddy Bear Bread memorabilia is available, including buttons, celluloid flags, and wrappers, the bears themselves are quite rare and unusual.

The frequency with which Teddy Bear Bakery memorabilia is found at many locations across the country suggests a franchise or a shared name, trading on the teddy's turn-of-the-century popularity.

Advertising cards designed by W.W. Denslow were collected in sets of four (a full set told the story of a bear finding and selling a loaf of bread) and could be traded in for a teddy bear stick pin.

New England Bakery of Pawtucket, Rhode Island, also made Teddy Bear Bread in two sizes — a five cent and a 10 cent loaf.

Teddy Bear bread advertisement, circa 1910.

A page from The Teddy Bears Baking School.

The Teddy Bears Baking School were premiums from The Fleischmann Co.

Teddy Bear bread advertisement.

Bimbo Bear Bread

Bimbo Bear is the symbol of a well-known Spanish bakery, similar, according to one spokesman, to Hostess Breads and Pastries in this country. Bimbo is featured on the wrappers of a whole range of breads and cakes and has represented his company on Spanish national television. The company is based in Barcelona.

Bimbo Bread and Pastries truck with Bimbo logo from Barcelona, Spain, courtesy of Mary Ann Johnstone Collection.

1942 advertisement for Lysol from the Woman's Home Companion. *Note the reference for a free "War-time Manual for Housewives."*

When the novelty wears off a baby...

SOMEWHERE ALONG THE LINE a baby stops being a miracle and becomes a person.

You suddenly realize that you no longer need tiptoe fearfully to the crib side to see whether he is still breathing.

The months have made him into a pretty dependable member of the family—no longer a bundle of worry marked "fragile" but someone to romp with and enjoy.

Yet often the fact that a baby outgrows infanthood, with its constant and complex threats, makes the pre-school years a neglected interval. Just because the child keeps on growing, it is easy to think that he no longer needs the help of the doctor except in cases of emergency.

That is a serious mistake—for many dangers lurk in these "in-between" years that bridge the gap from babyhood to kindergarten. Your child's heart...lungs...eyes should be watched by someone alert to any hint of trouble. Tonsils and adenoids may cause difficulties. Defects in posture may be leading soft little bones to take shapes that will be all wrong in later years.

These, and other problems of bodily growth, make it vitally important that the doctor see the child at regular intervals. These examinations give your doctor a chance to discover trouble before it becomes deep-rooted. They are an important check on a child's diet, habits and condition.

And they also let the physician carry out a program of immunization against communicable diseases your child will encounter when he starts school.

Seeing the doctor regularly during these pre-school years is the soundest possible way of making certain that your child will enter the "larger world" with a head start instead of a handicap.

PARKE, DAVIS & COMPANY
Detroit, Michigan

*The World's Largest Makers of
Pharmaceutical and Biological Products*

See your doctor

Parke, Davis & Company advertisement from 1940.

Below: *The Big Baer Cigar advertisement.*

M. Born & Co., a Chicago tailor, advertisement.

Amberol Records advertisement from 1908.

Below: *The little girl from the Amberol Records advertisement seated with her teddy bear.*

At the Christmas Matinee

The greatest improvement in sound-reproducing instruments was made when Mr. Edison invented AMBEROL Records

No one thing has added so much to the pleasure of the Edison Phonograph as a Record which plays more than four minutes, and reproduces the melody or voice so clearly and perfectly that the illusion almost defies detection.

Edison Amberol Records are the same size as the ordinary Edison Records. They can be played upon any Edison Phonograph by the addition of an attachment which any dealer can supply and any dealer can affix.

Longer selections are now available for the Edison Phonograph than have ever been available before for any sound-reproducing machine, and these selections are better given.

No Edison Phonograph outfit is complete without the attachment to play Edison Amberol Records.

You can hear these new Records at any dealer's. Learn about the attachment and equip your Phonograph with it today. If you haven't an Edison Phonograph, you can now buy one which plays both styles of Records—the two-minute and four-minute.

NATIONAL PHONOGRAPH CO., 60 Lakeside Avenue, Orange, New Jersey

The Edison Business Phonograph saves the time of high-salaried men and increases their letter-writing capacity.

[1908]

A&W Root Beer Bear

The A&W Root Beer Bear, 13in (33cm) tall, wears an orange jacket and cap marked on the chest with an A&W patch. He was first offered as a premium by A&W Root Beer, a subsidiary of United Brands, in 1975. He cost $3.95 at participating root beer stands. A plush hand puppet was sold for $1.00 the following year. The costumed version has appeared in parades and conventions, and a cartoon version was briefly seen on television. This very difficult to find item has a value of $50.

A&W Root Beer bear.

A&W Root Bear advertisement.

A&W Root Bear Hand Puppet offer.

One Bear for the Road

Bear Automotive Service Equipment Company, headquartered in Milwaukee, Wisconsin, was founded in 1917 by brothers Will and Henry Dammann. Here again, the original owners chose the bear as the company symbol simply because they liked it.

Although this corporate logo has never been put out in stuffed form, the "Bear Alignment" sign, displaying a friendly yellow cub with high-set ears, big grin, and paw extended in welcome, has been visible at roadside garages and gas stations since the 1920s.

the FACTS of Life
make BEAR SIGNS everywhere

1. It's 3 to 1 your car is out of alinement.
2. Only 1/8th inch misalinement can waste 50% tire life. Misalinement causes hard steering, dangerous vibration.
3. It all adds up to wear on vital parts, driver fatigue and costly accidents.

the SIGNS of Life
for you and your car

get your Free
**INSTANT Steering
CHECK-UP TODAY.**

At THE SIGN of the HAPPY BEAR — YOU'LL FIND HIM NEARLY EVERYWHERE, wherever cars are serviced... car dealers, garages and service stations including these and many other retail service centers where Bear Equipment is used:

J. C. Penney Co., Inc.

Western Auto Supply Co.

OK Tire Stores

U.S. Royal Tires

Fisk Tires

Gillette Tires

Ameron Corporation

Woolco Department Stores

Midas, Inc.

White Stores

Abel Label in Dept. Stores

FREE

FREE HONEST-TO-GOODNESS GENUINE 4 LEAF CLOVER KEY CHAINS... As a reminder that the Lucky Driver drives a Bear Safety Tested Car. MAIL THIS COUPON TO the sponsor of this safety message. BEAR MFG. CO., Dept. L M, Rock Island, Ill.

In Canada: Bear Equipment and Services Ltd., Toronto

Published in behalf of Bear Service Shops Everywhere by, the World Leader in Automotive Safety Test Equipment

Bear Safety Service advertisement from April 2, 1965, Life magazine.

Opposite Page: *Neponset Woolen Mills sportswear advertisement from March 1947 Holiday magazine.*

Behr Manning advertisements for Barney sandpaper were paper bears with many versatile outfits.

59

ASK DADDY TO USE THE SANDPAPER WITH
"BARNEY" IN THE TRIANGLE

ASK DADDY TO USE THE SANDPAPER WITH "BARNEY" IN THE TRIANGLE

QUALITY ABRASIVES

BEHR - MANNING   TROY, N.Y., U.S.A

LITHO IN U.S.A

Prize in a Box

A set of 16 postcards featuring the Cracker Jack Bears was designed by B.E. Moreland and published in 1907. When offered, you could get the entire set free for 10 side panels, or 10 cents and one side panel, from the manufacturer, Rueckheim Brothers and Eckstein of Chicago, Illinois.

One bear was light brown and the other dark brown, in a style very similar to the then newly popular fictional bears, Teddy B and Teddy G.

This premium was offered during the "golden age" of advertising postcards, from 1898 to 1918. Slightly smaller than standard postcards, these collectibles featured rhyming verses, such as:

"Oh, Mr. Teddy, drop your gun,
For us such business is no fun.
So please don't keep us on the rack,
'Cause we're the bears with Cracker Jack."

Cracker Jack Bears postcards are from 1907.

A current Cracker Jack prize.

True Blue Teddy

A 1987 study by psychologist Dr. Paul Horton of Meriden, Connecticut, found that teddy bears are American childhood's first "solacing object," ranking right after parents for 60 percent of the United States' population.

"Teddy bears are close enough in their general configuration to a human — outstretched arms, a gentle gleam in their eyes — to have an obvious potential to be a comforter, like a mother," says Horton.

"Over the past 100 years, children have been offered a lot of solaces — stuffed lions, giraffes, and so forth — but for some reason, children prefer the teddy bear.

"Part of it may be that the bear is enough like a human for the child to relate to it, but different enough to distinguish it. It's ideally situated in psychological space."[1]

Dogs and cats are the animals used most often in advertising. They have the advantage (depending on how you look

Berryman's bear joins Teddy Roosevelt in a 1930s cartoon.

at it) of being the animals who live most closely with man. Of course, dogs and cats are frequently used to advertise products for dogs and cats.

Bears occupy third place when it comes to animals used in advertising, but, after all, no one buys bear kibble, bear litter or bear flea collars, so there are no advertisements for bear products.

Bears, instead, are recognized as being both "people-like" and noble. Monkeys and apes are also "people-like," but they are not big in advertising because of the perceived insulting connotation. Lions and tigers are noble, but they are the kings of beasts, and not the least "people-like."

Bears walk on two legs (sometimes), are fiercely protective of their young, have a well-known sweet tooth, and have a lumbering, almost clownish gait. Everything about them seems tailor-made to appeal to humans. Who would not believe any endorsement given by a true blue teddy?

[1]*The Solace Paradigm*, International Universities Press, Dr. Paul Horton, 1988.

Roosevelt campaign bear based upon the "teddy bear" of Clifford Berryman's famous cartoons.

*Sears, Roebuck and Co. advertisement for the new Winnie the Pooh collection of Perma-Prest®
clothes from the November 1968 issue of* McCall's.

*Sears, Roebuck and Co. Winnie the Pooh Centennial Bear marked 100 years of Sears. Other Poohs
are, left to right, early 1960s Sears Pooh, the 1986 Centennial Pooh in a limited edition, a small
British-made 2in (5cm) Pooh from the English Pavilion at EPCOT™ Center, Walt Disney World®,
and Pooh circa 1980 from Sears, a little fatter but more to love.*

Above: *Hidy and Howdy were the mascots for the XV Olympic Winter Games in Calgary.*

Left: *Ovaltine postcard drawn by Phyllis Cooper.*

Poor Teddy has caught a cold,
We left him out all night.
But when he's had some OVALTINE.
I'm sure he'll be all right.

To Be a Bear or
Not To Be a Bear,
That is the Question

The word "panda" is a French corruption of a Tibetan term meaning bamboo eater. Although the debate continues as to where the panda's lineage belongs, he arguably looks like a bear.

In 1928, Kermit and Theodore Roosevelt Jr. mounted an expedition to China to hunt giant pandas, and brought back a stuffed specimen to their father, President Teddy Roosevelt.

Finally, in 1934, Ruth Harkness, wife of the late naturalist William Harkness, brought the first live panda cub out of China to New York's Bronx Zoo.

Ling-Ling and Hsing-Hsing who arrived at Washington D.C.'s National Zoo in the 1970s are not only zoo stars and an inspiration to the stuffed toy industry, they are diplomats of the first rank. With the help of the World Wildlife Fund (which uses the panda as its symbol), China and the United States have cooperated in joint research on these elusive creatures, providing intriguing information about their anatomical, medical and reproductive behavior. This co-operation is a first step to international friendship, where before, only suspicion existed. Certainly, the National Zoo pandas could serve as a warm and welcome symbol of worldwide peace. Perhaps they will someday.

Stuffed panda by Sun and Star Co., Ltd., copyright Fun & Fancy Products, Mill Valley, California, which was made in Japan. This is sold at the National Zoo Gift Shop to visitors. 9¹/₂in (24cm) tall in a sitting position, the panda is black and white plush with brown plush paws, glasene eyes, black felt nose and has a cloth tag.

Real Bears

The bear family is related to the raccoon (Procyonidae) to which the panda family (Ailurus fulgens) also belongs. The largest member of the panda family, the giant panda, is called Ailuropoda melanoleuca. "Uro" and "Arcto" are both words meaning bear. In China, pandas are called "beishung" meaning the white bear. In that Oriental country, stuffed replicas of pandas are treated like teddy bears.

The koala from Australia is named Phascolarctos cinereous, the "arctos" meaning bear-like. In Australia, the tree bear or native sloth, as it is also called, can be found as a stuffed toy which is played with exactly as teddy bears are in this country.

From Ice Age art to Winnie-the-Pooh, bears have been familiar symbols. Everyone loves them. They are big. They are strong. They are powerful. Yet, they appear gentle and friendly, sometimes almost clownish. Some of their traits mimic human behavior to a startling degree.

Among the more familiar bears are the polar bear (ursus maritimus), sloth bear (melursus ursinus), spectacled bear (tremarctos ornatus) and the grizzly bear (ursus horribilis).

Bear to the Throne

In the meantime, bears are hard at work as the symbol for FONZ, Friends of the National Zoo. The panda pair have become such celebrities that their mating rituals get front page headlines, and round-the-clock volunteer birth-watches are periodically held at the National Zoo. If Ling-Ling and Hsing-Hsing ever produce a cub, he will be an instant American hero, as much of an "heir to the throne" in this country as Prince William was a few years back in England.

Zoo Ambassadors

Some real bears become symbols of companies or causes. In the case of the National Zoo pandas in Washington, D.C., two unassuming animals, Ling-Ling and Hsing-Hsing, have come to represent international friendship.

The endangered panda appears occasionally in ancient Chinese children's literature, but was first discovered by the West in 1869, when missionary Pere David captured a specimen, which was, unfortunately, killed. He named the species ursus melanoleucus (black-and-white bear). In Paris, Director of the French Museum of Natural History, Alphonse Milne-Edwards, decided the specimen (which had been shipped to him by David) was anatomically nearer to raccoons and named it ailuropodus melanoleuca (cat-footed black-and-white animal).

Ling-Ling and Hsing-Hsing are the only giant pandas permanently residing in the United States. In 1972, former President Richard M. Nixon took an historic trip to the Peoples Republic of China, thawing a Cold War relationship that had lasted between the two countries for 30 years. As a result, China gifted the American people with a pair of giant pandas, the first to live in the United States since Pandah died at the Bronx Zoo in New York in 1951. (Pandah was a female without a mate. The last male panda in the United States, Happy, died in 1946.)

To Sleep, Perchance to Dream of Bears

TraveLodge stuffed Sleepy Bear, 13in (33cm) tall, brown plush, wearing attached orange felt sleep shirt and cap. Cap is marked "Sleepy." Orange plush feet, felt features, black pompom nose.

The first stuffed Sleepy Bear, circa 1967, was designed by Clayton Beaver, 12in (31cm) tall, and is brown plush with felt eyes and mouth and pompom nose. The night clothes are red or white flannel with the word "Sleepy" marked on the cap. It is valued at $60.

TraveLodge International's Sleepy Bear has been used as the motel chain's symbol since 1954. The first stuffed premium Sleepy Bear was offered in 1967, and a version of this stuffed bear is still available today.

The Sleepy Bear Club, organized in 1973, offers free membership, as well as buttons, t-shirts, rings and patches, to children staying at TraveLodges. A spokesperson for the hotel explains: "Sleepy Bear represents reliable comfort in a relaxing atmosphere and a nice place to stay."

TraveLodge started as a small California motel chain and based its mascot bear on the symbol of the State of California, a golden bear. With the addition of droopy eyelids and a night cap and shirt, the bear became known as "Sleepy."

The chain now operates throughout the United States and into Canada and Mexico, and the registered bear symbol is found on every piece of stationery, advertising, and other promotional material put out by TraveLodge.

The first stuffed Sleepy was designed by Clayton Beaver, a TraveLodge employee, in 1967, and was 12in (31cm) tall, brown plush, with felt eyes and mouth and pompon nose. The night clothes were red or white flannel with the word "Sleepy" marked on the cap. That original bear is considered highly collectible today and usually brings prices over $60 when sold at auctions and flea markets.

Sleepy is currently available in sizes ranging from 19½in (50cm) plush to 5½in (14cm) vinyl. Each bear is marked: "Sleepy Bear, TM TraveLodge International, Inc., copyright 1978, C.J. Beaver, Palm Springs, Ca." Sleepy is also available as a pajama bag and as a plush puppet.

The Sleepy symbol first appeared at the newly opened Bishop, California, TraveLodge in 1954, shown as a graphic full-face cartoon, with one paw and leg extended in a suggestion of sleepwalking. He was also made into a costume that could be used in parades and openings of new facilities, such as the first out-of-state motel in Tacoma, Washington, in 1956. It was in Washington State in 1956, in fact, that Sleepy was first seen on television. Now, of course, he is a star!

Above: *Sleepy Bear rocks a baby to sleep in the original early 1960s costume.* Photograph courtesy of TraveLodge International.

TraveLodge was honored in 1972 by the James B. Beam Distilling Co. when Sleepy Bear was selected to be cast in china, thus becoming one of that company's prestigious collector's bottles. Photograph courtesy of Mille Ann Natale.

Right: *American Heart Association Heart-to-Heart® bear made my Chosun. For each bear purchased, Chosun made a donation to the American Heart Association.*

Heart donor.

He's the Heart-To-Heart Bear. The bear with the beating heart. And right now you can help him in the fight against heart disease and stroke When you buy a Heart-To-Heart Bear, Chosun will make a donation to the American Heart Association. And that'll do your heart good.

HEART-TO-HEART BEAR
BY CHOSUN

Official Sponsor of 🛡️ American Heart Association

Where There is Smoke, There is Smokey

Smokey Bear was created in 1942 when concern about possible Japanese shelling of the California coast caused worry about widespread forest fires. The United States Department of Agriculture [USDA] Forest Service organized the Cooperative Forest Fire Prevention campaign and joined with the Wartime Advertising Council to choose a representative symbol.

A bear was chosen and first depicted by Albert Staehle, an artist famous for the cocker spaniels he painted for national magazine covers. The bear was named "Smokey" after Smokey Joe Martin, Assistant Fire Chief of New York City from 1919 to 1930. The famous message, "Only YOU Can Prevent Forest Fires," was created in 1947. By 1952, Smokey was so well known that Congress passed the Smokey Bear Act, allowing the Forest Service to license the use of Smokey and use the royalties for fire prevention.

In 1984, Smokey celebrated his 40th birthday, and the United States Department of Agriculture issued a special booklet (Forest Service FS-390) to mark the occasion. It is a retrospective of fire prevention posters, beginning in 1939, with Smokey making his first official ap-

The official Smokey Bear costume of the Forest Service is shown in an official pose.

pearance in 1944. In 1972 and 1982, guest stars appeared on the Smokey posters: Snoopy and Bambi. They are fictional characters. But six years after he was created, Smokey became a real bear.

In 1950 a cub was rescued from a forest fire in the Lincoln National Forest

Miscellaneous Smokey Bear advertisements from 1944 to 1984.

in New Mexico. The badly burned bear was found clinging to a blackened tree and was taken to a nearby ranger station where he was nursed back to health.

When he was fully recovered, he was sent to live in the National Zoo in Washington, D.C., where he has remained as a living symbol. In 1956, the ever-popular Smokey was given his own ZIP code — 20252 — to help in processing all his fan mail. The USDA Forest Service considers Smokey its most effective spokesperson: in 1942, ten million acres of forest were burned. By 1981, that number was reduced to three million.

The first Smokey Bear stuffed toy was made, naturally, by Ideal Toys, makers of the first American teddy

Center, 8½in (22cm) Smokey bubble bath container from the 1950s held 11 ounces of Colgate-Palmolive bubble bath. Smaller Smokeys are 1960s salt and pepper shakers, courtesy Millie Natale Collection.

bears. Available in 1952, each bear came with an application to be a Junior Forest Ranger.

Although the original Smokey passed away, he has been replaced in the National Zoo with Smokey, Mark II. Smokey also continues to appear in costume at classrooms, at parades and at public events, as well as on public service announcements on television. Middle age has not dimmed his vigor for protecting the forests that all bears love so well.

Replica of a 20 cent stamp.

Hamm's beer coaster.

A poster for Hamm's beer featuring their trademark bear.

21in (53cm) black and white plush stuffed bear with Hamm's beer label sewn on his chest. He has a large black pompom nose, black on white plastic eyes, and red felt tongue, top knot of black shag, zipper compartment at his back for a small radio. Cloth tag reads: "Distributed by Stephen Distributing Co., Minneapolis, Minn., manufactured by Fable Toy Co., N.Y." Valued at $65. Photograph courtesy of Marleen Wendt.

Hamm's beer advertisement.

Down Under

Billy Bluegum became an Australian national hero with the publication of *The Magic Pudding* by Norman Lindsay in 1918.

His first appearance, however, came in the Sydney *Bulletin* on August 11, 1904, around the same time that the teddy bear was born in the United States. In May 1907, the first issue of the monthly magazine *Lone Hand* was published. It featured a cartoon boxing match between Bill Wattleberry and Ginger Bluegum. This was the first appearance of the names Wattleberry and Bluegum, who became Bunyip Bluegum (later Billy) and his Uncle Wattlebury in *The Magic Pudding.*

According to Lindsay biographer Keith Wingrove, the name Billy Bluegum was first used in the January 1908 issue of *Lone Hand.* "From then on, Norman's bear was always known as Billy or Bill Bluegum, even though he is called Bunyip Bluegum in *The [Magic] Pudding.*"

Book covers of Norman Lindsay's book The Magic Pudding.

Bill frequently appeared in the pages of the *Bulletin*, and many Christmas issues featured a full page Billy Bluegum drawing. The last new drawing of the little koala appeared on December 12, 1956, and depicted Billy at the Olympic Games in Melbourne. He was an unofficial mascot, much as Misha was official mascot for the Moscow games and Hidy and Howdy took top honors for the Calgary Olympics.

Norman Alfred Lindsay (1879 to 1969) invested Billy and his companion koalas with distinctly human personalities and appearances. Billy became so popular, in fact, that stuffed koalas in Australia are sometimes referred to as billies rather than teddies. The bear was also used in advertisements for such diverse things as shoe polish and political campaigns.

Although some purists argue that a koala is not really a bear (and, indeed, it

8in (20cm) circa 1950s hard stuffed koala, made in Australia from kangaroo fur with leather paws and a plastic nose; no labels.

Norman Lindsay's Bears, *a selection by Keith Wingrove.*

is not), most teddy collectors have a few stuffed examples of these appealing animals. Commonly referred to as a bear in Australia, the koala is a small, appealing creature. As Ambrose Pratt wrote in *The Call of the Koala*, copyright 1937, Robertson & Mullins Limited, Melbourne:

"No more gentle, harmless, trustful, quaintly comical, wistfully curious, wise looking, pathetic and lovable little creature ever existed, and none with a face more subtly suggestive of some of the more endearing psychological qualities we are wont to regard as pertaining to the human race."

In fact, koalas have been as popular in advertising in Australia as bears have been in the rest of the world. For example, Dr. Blue Gum eucalyptus oil, with a koala on the label, was a popular remedy in 1916. Koala Kola ("the kooler kola") was actually mineral water first bottled around 1945, and used a koala as a trademark. Three koalas, stacked one on the other, were the trademark of Lewis Ornstien's sound records in 1958, and the Perdriau Rubber Company used a koala as the logo on its patent medicine, back in 1916. Gumlypta, an agricultural chemical first made in 1919, used a koala in a suit and top hat on its advertising, and Koala Jelly Crystals were a popular candy in the 1940s and 1950s.

An advertisement for the XVI Olympics in Melbourne, Australia. This 1956 advertisement was drawn by Norman Lindsay.

A TIME FOR CELEBRATION'

"Cobra," The Boot Polish
and The Floor Polish

Chunder Loo,
Of Akim Foo,
Sees to boots
And floorcloth too.

Where you note
A dazzling sheen,
There the "COBRA"
Bears have been.

Sitting proudly
On his throne,
Chunder says—
"It shines alone!"

Sun up high
And "COBRA" here
Rivals are
From year to year!"

A 1930s advertisement for Cobra boot and floor polish. The characters were drawn by Norman Lindsay.

PLEASE OBSERVE
VISITING HOURS

I'M A BOY!

ROOM _____

MY NAME

MY MOTHER _____

MY BIRTHDATE _____ TIME _____

BIRTH WEIGHT_____ LBS ___ OZ LENGTH ____ IN

HEAD____

MOTHER'S

MY DOCTO

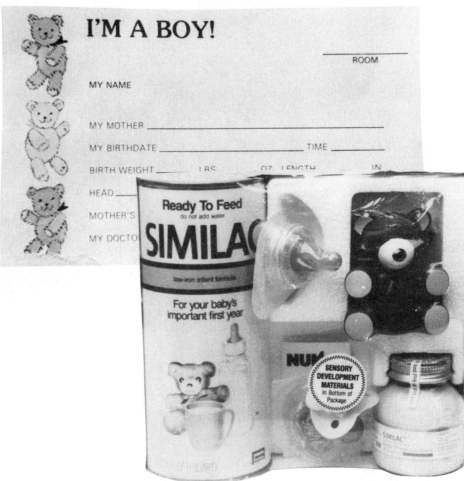

Ready To Feed
do not add water

SIMILAC

low-iron infant formula

For your baby's
important first year

SENSORY
DEVELOPMENT
MATERIALS
In Bottom of
Package

Miscellaneous hospital supplies with teddy bear themes including Similac® formula and infant care kit, Medi-pak® huggables™ electrodes for infant monitoring, a visiting hours sign based on the bear who looks identical to the Similac bear, and a newborn's identification tag for his bassinet.

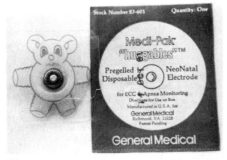

Stock Number 83-601   Quantity: One

Medi-Pak®
"huggables"®™

Pregelled   NeoNatal
Disposable   Electrode

for ECG & Apnea Monitoring
Directions for Use on Box
Manufactured in U.S.A. for
General Medical
Richmond, VA. 23228
Patent Pending

General Medical

Prestone anti-freeze advertisement from 1940.

The Victory over Cold!

TRY

TRAMRICK

IT'S GOOD

The Highball Favorite

Tramrick whiskey postcard.

"The Hall Mark of Gum Excellency"

Rastus is as black as jet,
Teddy white as snow,
What they both are talking of
Every one should know.

Rastus said to Teddy Bear
"What means that trade mark red?
I see it on your breast and arms,
Please tell me! Will you, Ted?"

"It means just this," said Teddy,
"That healthy you'll become,
If every day you'll chew with me
Listerated Pepsin Gum."

Listerated Pepsin Gum postcard.

L'ASPIRON
DÉPOUSSIÉREUR ÉLECTRIQUE

Sous la forme la plus pratique, le dépoussiéreur le plus efficace

L'ASPIRON par sa forme pratique et sa puissance d'aspiration est sans conteste le dépoussiéreur le plus efficace actuellement sur le marché.

Son prix raisonnable le met à la portée de toutes les Maîtresses de Maison soucieuses d'hygiène et d'économie.

Complet avec ses accessoires

780 frs.

Démonstration et vente chez tous les électriciens, magasins, etc.

ou

SOCIÉTÉ de PARIS et du RHONE
Constructeurs

33, Champs-Elysées, Paris

PARIS	LYON
33, Champs-Elysées	11, Qu. Jules-Courmont

L'Aspiron, a French vacuum cleaner, advertisement from 1927.

A Bear for All Reasons

Big business has thrown in with bears, using generic teddies in its advertising as symbols of warmth, honesty and security.

In a major departure from their practice of using photos of transportation equipment and terminals in their advertisements in *Forbes* and *Business Week*, Transway, a transportation and distribution company, used a teddy bear photograph in a 1981 advertisement. Although not offered as a premium, the bear proved so successful he has been used in many subsequent advertisements.

According to company spokesman Richard Mann: "We decided the widely accepted teddy bear would be a legitimate attention getter, and still be taken seriously. While we neither sell nor distribute teddy bears, our advertisements seem to be indisputable evidence of their popularity and drawing power."

As Bryan Holme said in his 1982 reference book, *Advertising: Reflections of a Century*: "Nothing is put in an advertisement just to take up space. Every image counts for something and says something."

All that is needed to convey a subtle message of warmth and caring in any kind of advertisement is the addition of a single teddy bear to the scene. And, of course, the advertisements themselves reflect our society.

As essayist Norman Douglas said in *South Wind* (Chapter 7, copyright 1917), "You can tell the ideals of a nation by its advertisements."

Advertisement for Behr Upright Pianos.

Why do they wear those Medals?

Because they are the ONLY "Upright Behrs"!

Below: *Cut-out for John Martin's thread. The head and backside were to be glued on the ends of spools of thread.*

Logo bears for Pan Am.

Pan American Pandas

Pierre Panda and his girlfriend Pam have been featured on Pan American Airlines advertising since 1977, symbolizing the global nature of the flight business. They were especially created for use in children's travel kids, given to youngsters boarding Pan Am international flights. Although not as closely associated with the Pan Am name as some advertising symbols, Pierre is extremely popular with young air travelers.

TEDDY BEAR

John Martin's SPOOL ZOO No 2

TEDDY BEAR SAYS

THIS is a BEAR—
a *Teddy* Bear.
Oh, how we love
to have him there!
He is so round,
so fat and funny.
And he likes candy,
cakes and honey.
YOU like them, too,
so I declare
You will be *friends*
with Teddy Bear.
Now, get a SPOOL,
and on each end
Paste Teddy BEAR,
your cozy FRIEND.

WITH your sharp scissors
cut me out carefully along
the fine dotted lines.
Now, get a SPOOL
of the right size to fit me.
Spread glue carefully on
both ends of the SPOOL,
allowing it to harden a
little; then stick my head
on one end of the
SPOOL and my tail end
on the other.
There, you have me
standing up for you as a
nice BEAR should do.

Right: *Carter's advertisement for play clothes from 1958.*

Carter's infant's sleeper advertisement from 1953.

On baby: "Sundowns" Sleeper. Safety-Step feet. Nevabind sleeve. Azure, mint, pink plaid. 6 mos.-4 yrs. $3.00.

How to be a fancy stepper

"Stepping out tonight?" asked Teddy when he saw my new plaid Carter's sleeper. "My, you have lots of evening clothes!" "That's because," I said, "everyone knows Carter's soft cotton knit sleepers make smart gifts for me—timesaving, no-iron gifts for Mother, too." Teddy twirled in front of the mirror, "I'd love to go to Dreamland, too, but I haven't a *thing* to wear! How do you get there?" "On my Safety-Step feet, of course! They'll get me there in a snap." Teddy counted the snaps on my Gro-Feature waist and laughed. "I think you'll get there in *four* snaps!" Isn't he a clever bear?

Carter's

THE WILLIAM CARTER CO., NEEDHAM HEIGHTS, MASS.

All are Carter-Set so won't shrink out of fit.

"Sundowns" Sleeper. Safety-Step feet. Neva-bind sleeve. Blue, pink, yellow Kitten print. 6 mos.-4 yrs. $3.00.

Acrilan "Jama-Blanket." Blanket-weight fabric. Safety-Step feet. Blue, pink, azure, yellow. S-M-L, $8.95. XL, $9.95.

An advertisement for Sunkist® oranges from the April 1927 issue of Ladies' Home Journal.

inset: *The little teddy bear looks on with sad eyes, waiting for his slice of orange.*

1946 advertisement for Schlitz beer.

Nashua Woolnap blanket advertisement. **inset:** *Little girl from the Nashua Woolnap blanket advertisement cuddles with her teddy.*

The Truth About Today's Refrigerators !

NO MATTER what reliable make of electric refrigerator you choose today, you'll get more value for your dollars than ever before.

★ FOR TODAY'S good electrical refrigerators are as fine an example of mechanical perfection as human ingenuity, skill, science and experience have produced. They're more than twice as efficient as the refrigerators of ten years ago, yet cost about one-half as much—so little that almost every family can afford the best in modern refrigeration.

★ WHATEVER make you choose, be sure to: (1) Get a refrigerator that's big enough for your family; too many of the early purchasers have wished for more storage space. (2) Get a refrigerator that's completely equipped—for the little conveniences become very, very important multiplied

over the years of use. (3) Get a refrigerator that's made by a reputable, experienced manufacturer, for actually it must outwear the mechanical life of many automobiles. (4) Ask your neighbors, shop carefully, and get all the facts, for you won't be buying a refrigerator again very soon if you choose wisely. (5) Remember that in refrigerators as in most other things, you get what you pay for—so the best model you can afford is your best investment.

★ NATURALLY we'd like to see you buy a General Electric, for we believe it's the finest machine ever built. Of course, we're prejudiced—but be sure you look at a G-E before you make up your mind.

★ MAYBE we build the G-E Refrigerator so well, because we have had a lot of experience... largest builder of electrical convenience

know that we offer, in this refrigerator, features tested by time and a mechanism that's just about tops in the engineering world.

★ G-E WAS FIRST with an all-steel cabinet—first with the sealed mechanism—first with many other vital improvements. Its record for low cost, dependable service is unsurpassed. And according to recent surveys it is *preferred by more people than any other refrigerator!* We try hard to give people their money's worth and to keep our prices low. A General Electric is priced no higher than other good refrigerators—as little as $114.95* buys a big 6 cu. ft. model. We believe G-E *actually costs less than any other refrigerator over the years!*

GENERAL EL

General Electric advertisement for a refrigerator from April 1941.

"List to the Tale of an Old Pine Table"

Fancy an ordinary kitchen table—five years old—selling for almost double its original cost after half a year on a roof top! And all because of a coat of Valspar Varnish-Stain!

Let Mrs. Frances Caplan of Brooklyn, N.Y., tell you in her own words how it happened.

"In order to keep my little son, who has a weak heart, away from excitement, and at the same time pleasantly occupied outdoors, I resurrected an old discarded kitchen table, Valsparred it, and in a cozy corner up on the roof Bobby and I played many a game on the nice shiny table. We had many a meal up there, too, and I taught him his A-B-C's.

"One day my husband came home and said we would have to sell our furniture as the office was planning to send him to Chicago for a several years' stay. We brought down the old table to hold the cut glass during the sale, intending to leave it in the rooms after everything was sold. You can imagine my astonishment when one woman asked me would I sell her the table. And all I had done to it after its long stay on the roof, exposed to the elements, was to wipe it off with a dust cloth!"

Mrs. Caplan's letter is only one of hundreds we have received telling of the great satisfaction given by Valspar Varnish-Stains. You, too, will find them invaluable in brightening up and making new again the woodwork and furniture about the house.

Valspar Varnish-Stains are Valspar itself plus beautiful, transparent stains. With one stroke of the brush you Valspar and stain, bringing out the full beauty of the grain.

These Varnish-Stains are ideal for finishing floors, furniture and all woodwork indoors and out. They are waterproof and accident-proof *and can be washed freely with hot water and soap*. They are easy to apply, dry dust free in 2 hours and hard overnight. The colors—Light Oak, Dark Oak, Walnut, Mahogany, Cherry and Moss Green.

Send in the coupon below for a sample can —enough to finish a small table or chair.

Send for Sample Can and Color Chart

Largest Manufacturers of High Grade Varnishes in the World

VALENTINE'S
VALSPAR
VARNISH-STAIN

This Coupon is worth 20 to 60 Cents

VALENTINE & COMPANY, 460 Fourth Ave., New York

Valentine's Valspar Varnish-Stain advertisement from 1926 with teddy bear in the foreground.

Right: Teddy bear from Valspar advertisement with Valspar spelled out in the blocks.

This 1917 painting was done by Henry F. Weirman for Cream of Wheat. The girls' teddy and doll both bow their heads when "Saying Grace."

© Corn Products Refining Co.

...AVE CANDY?

...rgy food. Most candy ...hich is food energy in ...vailable form, along ...ilk products and eggs. ...candy in reasonable ...right time is a valuable ...nutrition at all ages. ...g candy, remember to ...dextrose on the label.

You will also find mention of dextrose on the labels of soft drinks, jams and jellies, ice creams and ices, canned fruits and juices, cereals and many other food products to which dextrose gives improved flavor, texture and appearance.

dextrose
FOOD-ENERGY SUGAR

This 1946 advertisement for dextrose from Corn Products Refining Co. extols the virtue of sugar in the diet of children. Note the girl's very American teddy.

Richardson's Products used the polar bear theme in 1948 to convey to readers the coolness of their mints. This advertisement features three mints: after dinner mints, jelly-filled after dinner mints and old-fashioned creamy mints.

Richardson's 1949 advertisement for after dinner mints.

1947 Welch's advertisement with two young girls and their toys enjoying a tea party.

inset: *The teddy bear which is somewhat hidden by one girl's elbow in the Welch's advertisement.*

This *Prudential Cook Book* included a calendar for 1910 and 1911 and first aid hints.

Green Giant peas advertisement from 1953.

Hydrox cookies advertisement from 1956.

Right: *1954 advertisement for Jell-O® brand gelatin dessert from* The Saturday Evening Post.

1954 advertisement for Jell-O® brand pudding and pie filling.

THE EIGHT AS BUICK BUILDS IT

Safe, Comfortable, Dependable
... the favorite fine car of modern women

The wide preference among women for the new Buick Eight leads to a natural question: "Why do more than half of all women who buy eights priced between $1000 and $2000 choose Buick?"

Safety, doubtless, receives early consideration. Thinking less of themselves, perhaps, than of their children, many women favor Buick because of the reliability of the Buick Valve-in-Head engine, the sturdiness of Buick's bodies by Fisher, the effectiveness of Buick's four-wheel brakes and the extra safety afforded by Buick's silent-shift Syncro-Mesh transmission.

Comfort is another deciding factor—especially the luxurious comfort which Buick offers in Fisher bodies insulated like a fine home against heat, cold and noise.

And, of course, most women realize how completely they can depend upon the all-round performance of the new Buick Eight. Thousands of women feel perfectly safe in making long trips alone in their Buicks, for Buick reliability is almost a tradition in American homes today.

These qualities, we believe, have made the new Buick Eight the favorite fine car of modern women.

Owing to their popularity, the present models of 1931 Buick Straight Eights will be continued throughout the coming summer and fall.

The new Buick Straight Eights, in four series and four price ranges, are offered in 22 luxurious models, from $1025 to $2035, f. o. b. Flint, Michigan. Consider the delivered price as well as the list price when comparing motor car values.

A   G E N E R A L   M O T O R S   V A L U E

BODY BY FISHER

WHEN BETTER AUTOMOBILES ARE BUILT, BUICK WILL BUILD THEM

A bear symbolizes safety and comfort in this 1931 automobile advertisement from Buick.

The eatingest youngsters
just happen to eat Post Sugar Crisp

For breakfast it's dandy—for snacks it's so handy.

The darling of the eating set. Plump puffs of muscle-building wheat, sparkled with sugar 'n' honey. Solid with nourishment.

KELLOGG'S INVITES THE KIDS TO MAKE THE ADS

YOU CAN GIVE MY PORRIDGE TO GOLDILOCKS, MOMMA... I WANT SOME KELLOGG'S CORN FLAKES!

FRESH FROM KELLOGG'S OF BATTLE CREEK

the CRISP, CRISP flakes with the DEEP, DEEP flavor!

...just a little bit better!

Above: *1959 advertisement for Post Sugar Crisp cereal.*

Left: *June 1953 advertisement for Kellogg's Corn Flakes that was written by Donna Hall of Gladewater, Texas, during a contest for young people to write Kellogg's advertisements.*

96

Left: *Early Post Sugar Crisp Bear from 1951.*

Post Super Sugar Crisp Bear trademark logo of 1980.

Below: *Remy's Oats bears circa 1920s.*

Below: *Domino Sugar offered this 15in (38cm) bear as a premium in 1975 for $2.98. The bear wore a yellow felt tie with the Domino Sugar name on it and was a replica of the costumed Domino bear who entertained visitors to the Six Flags recreation parks. Courtesy Millie Natale Collection.*

Kellogg's 1985 Honey Smacks cereal box.

Cook's Rice advertisement which offered a teddy bear cut-out with the purchase of two boxes is circa 1920.

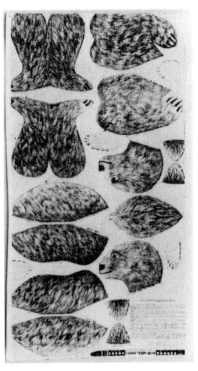

Warmth at the Heart of an Icee Bear

The Icee trademark polar bear was first used in 1964, primarily as a costumed figure at sales promotions and business conventions. In 1968, it was first offered as a plush toy and is still available. The design is basically unchanged. The bear is 19in (48cm) tall, white plush, with droopy black felt eyes and a black plush nose. He wears a red, non-removable shirt with a big letter "I" on it.

The Icee Corporation, which also makes popcorn, frozen cola, soft frozen ice cream and yogurt and soft pretzels, has frequently used the bear on national radio and television commercials. Company correspondence is, in fact, signed with a distinctive paw print!

Icee was first developed in 1959 as a frozen carbonated soft drink. Syrup, carbon dioxide and water under pressure were mixed in a freezing chamber. The soft drink is served toothpaste fashion into red, white and blue paper cups. Past slogans include: "You don't drink, you slurp through a straw!" and "It doesn't pour...it chuckles into the cup."

Icee has available a line of "Bear Point Treasures," including beach towels, magnets, frisbees, t-shirts, banks and stuffed bears, all with the bear logo inscribed. These can be obtained by saving the Icee Bear points found on all sizes of Icee cups. The redeemable prizes have proved very popular and can be purchased with points only, or a combination of cash and points. A 2½in (6cm) magnet, for example, costs 100 bear points, or three bear points and $1.00.

According to spokesperson Jackie Carter at National Icee Corporation headquarters in Philadelphia, Pennsylvania, the bear was chosen as a symbol by the original owners — John E. Mitchell Co. because they found the bear appealing.

Icee bear premium is a 16in (41cm) white plush bear with a sewn-on red flannel shirt with a vinyl "I" of the front and Icee Bear vinyl patch on the back. His eyes are black plastic with white felt eyelids, his mouth is black felt, and his nose is black shag plush. Attached paper tag reads "Christy Mfg. Co., Fayetteville, N.C."

An Embearrassment of Riches

A 1986 article in Adweek's *Marketing Week* claimed "you can bearly open a newspaper anywhere in the U.S. and not come upon an advertisement offering a cuddly teddy at a discount (or even free) if you spend a specified sum on other goods."[1]

Offers the writer spotted in the Philadelphia area that year included:

1) Spend $60 at John Wanamaker's department store and became eligible to buy a *Rudi Bear* (a $25 value) for $12.

2) Spend $35 at Bradlee's Department Store, and buy a *Bradlee's Christmas Bear* for $10.

3) Spend $50 in Bloomingdale's and buy a Gund-made *Bloomie Bear* for $10.95.

4) Spend $50 at Filene's and buy *Feelix Bear* for $12.

5) Spend $50 at I. Magnin, and buy a bear for $10.95 (free if you spend $150).

6) Spend $50 at Dayton Hudson Department Store and get a *Santabear* for $10.

7) Buy a Frigidaire refrigerator and receive a free *Frigi-Bear*.

8) Buy Fila brand sportswear and get a free Fila's *Fitness Bear*.

Other examples of this trend would be: Lord and Taylor's *Christmas Bear*, Woodward and Lothrop's *Kringle Bear*, J.C. Penney's *Christmas Bear*, Burlington Industries *Burlie Bears*, and Nichol's *Nicky Bear*.

Bear promotionals work. People move their accounts from bank to bank in their quest for a free bear, or they explore a new store, one where they have never shopped before, just to earn the chance to buy a special promotional teddy.

"Why did so many merchandisers decide that the bear was the animal with the right stuffing to attract customers? Why not a puppy or a kitten or a wooly lamb? The answer is that the bear is king of the plush animal jungle. According to the Toy Manufacturer's Association, some 90 million plush toys (retail value more than $500 million) are sold annually. One industry insider says that, usually, at least half will be bears."[1]

Neil Friedman, vice president of soft toys for Hasbro Industries, credits the bear's popularity to "tradition." Whatever the reason, it is still a bull market for bears and for everything with which they are associated. As Friedman says, "Just about any concept will sell better with a bear."

[1] "Retailers Say Teddy's the Season's Bear Necessity," Adweek's *Marketing Week*, Dec. 16, 1986, Rose DeWolf

Misha

The *Misha* family of bears comes in sizes ranging from 8in to 25in (20cm to 64cm). He was created as mascot for the 1980 Summer Olympic Games in Moscow and produced in stuffed versions by both Russia and R. Dakin & Co. in the United States.

President Carter's announcement of the American boycott of the games temporarily left *Misha*, a brown plush bear, with plastic eyes and nose, and felt paws, in the lurch. Dakin had already sold 75,000 of the creatures in their colorful, five-ring-buckle Olympic belt, with an official Olympic cloth tag. With 100,000 bears still in stock, Dakin attempted to "Americanize" the teddy, by removing the belt, cutting the cloth tag in half, and adding a patriotic tee-shirt (which, in one case, read "I'm just a bear!")

But, as any teddy bear at the center of international politics is bound to do, *Misha* rose above it all to become a highly sought after collectible in his original Olympic garb.

More properly called "Mishka," Misha has been a favorite character in Russian folklore since the 12th century and is based on the popular, live performing bears in traveling Russian circuses. A recent Mishka cartoon bear has appeared on Russian television, and teddy bears are generally called mishkas in the Soviet Union.

Misha, *the 10in (25cm) Olympic mascot bear from Dakin with Russian stacking dolls.*

The first personal banker for kids.

(Household Banker Bear Club℠ makes saving fun and educational.)

When it comes to saving money, kids should do more than grin and bear it. That's why we've created Household Banker Bear, to make saving fun.

Just bring in the kids and open up a savings account for as little as $10.00. (That's an amount other banks find too small to be bear-able. But at Household Bank we think families and individuals— even kids—are sweet as honey.)

Ten dollars establishes an interest bearing savings account, and earns your child a membership in the Household Banker Bear Savings Club. Kids get their own passbook and a free subscription to the quarterly Banker Bear

newsletter, filled with educational games, stories, riddles and puzzles.

Each dollar they deposit earns a Banker Bear Buck which can be used to buy stuffed Banker Bears and other special rewards.

America's Family Bank
Household Bank
A FEDERAL SAVINGS BANK

EQUAL HOUSING LENDER

Downtown Baltimore: 16 E. Lombard Street; Brooklyn Park: 400 Ritchie Highway; Catonsville: 609 Frederick Road; Dundalk: 009 Merritt Boulevard; Lutherville: 1700 York Road; Severna Park: 563 Ritchie Highway; Woodlawn: 5512 Baltimore National Pike; Woodlawn: 1700 North Rolling Road.

CALL: 244-0110
TDD 752-7010
For Hearing and Speech Impaired.

Above: Household Bank advertisement from 1989 which offered Household Banker Bear for opening a child's account with only $10.

Bear necessities

Take us home for the holidays!

A honey of an offer

Get a teddy bear when you open either of two checking plans with Meridian Bank.

There are two Meridian Bears to choose from, each 17 inches high. With the holidays drawing near, Meridian Bears make adorable gifts for anyone.

Your Meridian Bear is free when you open a Checking for Savers or a Market Rate Checking Plan with a deposit of $1000 or more. Our Checking for Savers Plan links a regular checking account with a savings account. There are no service charges when you maintain a minimum daily balance of $300.

As for our Market Rate Checking Plan, it links an Interest Checking Account with a Market

Rate Savings Account. Earn high interest with no service charges when you maintain a minimum daily balance of $1000.

Both of these accounts also come with a nice extra—a Meridian Card. It lets you access your accounts 24 hours a day at any of 135 Meridian Card Centers℠ and any MAC® or PLUS System® location.

The bear facts

Meridian Bears are a limited edition. When they become extinct, the offer ends.

So don't hibernate. Visit any Meridian Bank branch office soon and open your account. Or you can purchase Meridian Bears for $15 each plus tax.

Meridian Bank
Professionals with the personal touch.

Meridian Bank advertisement from 1989 which offers bears as a premium for opening a new account of $1000 or more.

WHILE passing through a wood one day,
A train was wrecked and, strange to say,
Some IVORY SOAP consigned to town
Was scattered through the forest brown.
Then wolves and foxes, bears and all,
Soon gathered round a water-fall.
Said they, "We often heard it said,

'It has no equal in the trade';
While men of science and of art
Pronounced it pure in every part.
But here, at last, we found an hour
To prove indeed its cleansing power;
And while the IVORY SOAP we find,
Be sure we'll use no other kind!"

The cakes of Ivory Soap are so shaped that they may
be used entire for general purposes, or divided with a stout
thread into two perfectly formed cakes for Toilet Use.

A 1902 Ivory Soap advertisement features bears who happen upon a train wreck where boxes of Ivory Soap have fallen off.

Opposite Page: *Advertisement for The International Fur Store. The cape design is circa 1890s.*

THE INTERNATIONAL FUR STORE

163 & 165 REGENT STREET

"Fur Capes will again be a prevailing fashion during the coming season."
SEALSKIN JACKETS and FUR CAPES of every description at
Wholesale Prices.

THE INTERNATIONAL FUR STORE,
163 and 165, REGENT STREET.

A Hershey Bears mascot teddy bear wears the team colors of maroon and white.

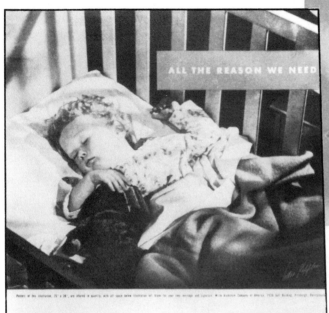

ALL THE REASON WE NEED

Once you've figured out that the main idea of this war is to give your Mary, and our Harry, the right, for always and always, to go to sleep unafraid . . . why then, you just naturally do better than your best. That's how sixty thousand of us here at Alcoa Aluminum have the thing sized up. This outfit of ours has built and is still building the greatest plants you ever saw. We've got the know-how and we're giving it away freely to other Americans. We're plugging at our end of it, hammer and tongs, three shifts a day, eight days a week. We've been doing that for over two solid years. This outfit really got going early. That's why you're reading so soon about thousands of planes a month. Get ready, folks; to read about your ten thousands. Because tomorrow we're breaking the record we set today.

The men and women of ALCOA ALUMINUM

HERSHEY **Bears**

Hershey Bears logo.

Above: *Alcoa Aluminum advertisement from the 1940s.*

softness?
you'll love me.

Fabric Softener

Snuggle

Right: *Snuggle bear premium offered by Lever Brothers.*

104

Good, Better, Best Bear

Good Bears of the World, headquartered in Hawaii, is an international charity dedicated to giving teddies to children and other needy persons, especially those in hospitals and institutions. The group was established in 1969 by Jim Ownby, and puts out a quarterly journal, called *Bear Tracks*, where the logo shows "Goody," the Good Bears mascot, against a global background.

The masthead of the journal states the group's goals thusly: "The Good

Good Bears of the World logo from the quarterly journal Bear Tracks.

Bears of the World is a non-profit USA IRS tax-exempt association, believing in love and friendship, with understanding. One of the primary goals of GBW is to provide teddy bears as comfort for children of all ages in hospitals, institutions and generally everywhere."

Without doubt, that is a sweeping statement, but also a hopeful one. As Bearo #1, Ownby said, "We preach the merits of Teddy Bearism, and it just might be one of the ways we can bridge the waters of turmoil that surround us."

Many Goody Bears have been given to those in need by Good Bear Dens all over the country.

Goody, the Good Bears of the World mascots that are distributed throughout the world through the organization. The bear was first produced in 1981 by Ideal. The 11in (28cm) bear is non-jointed and made of tan plush. His tag reads "copyright Ideal Toy Corporation, 1981, made in Taiwan." After Ideal folded, Dakin took over the making of Goody *in 1984. This is also an 11in (28cm) bear with a lighter tan plush. His tag reads "Good Bears of the World trademark, Product of R. Dakin & Co., Product of Taiwan." Both bears have yarn noses, glasene eyes and cream colored paws that are outstretched.*

The Chicago Bears Bear is a 26in (66cm) tan plush bear with a non-removable white flannel football jersey logoed with the Chicago Bears football helmet. The face and inner ears are yellow plush, the nose is black plush, the eyes are black plastic on white vinyl backings and the mouth has a red flannel tongue. The cloth tag attached to the left foot reads "Windy, Manufactured exclusively for the First National Bank of Chicago, Chicago's Bank, Animal Fair, Inc., copyright 1978, Chanhassen, Minn."

Current World Wildlife Fund trademark and logo.

Logo from a young woman's magazine in Japan, Heibon-Sha.

British shoe manufacturer's logo.

State of California logo bear.

Yosemite National Park logo.

Grizzly brand scroll saw advertisement.

Premier

Premier Ice, a logo of a Danish company.

TravAlaska Tours logo.

Calol, symbol for the Standard Oil Company of California.

106

Bear Automotive logo.

The CHOC (Children's Hospital of Orange County, Calif.) logo, an injured teddy bear, is called "Choco."

Spain's current Bimbo Bear logo for a popular brand of bread.

White Bear Soap Powder panel from a circa 1920s Swedish advertisement.

Bear Brand Hosiery logo.

This thumbs-up teddy appears on the side panel on a box of disposable diapers from Italy, circa 1989.

Logo for the city of Berlin.

Left, the original logo for Bear Drinking Straws, and right, the current logo.

Chicago Bears logo.

Bear Brand nylons advertisement.

Logo bear from a German milk company.

Merrill-Lynch bull logo.

Manza Kanko Hotel, a Japanese hotel, logo.

Logo from an photography magazine published in Finland, Unsikuvalenti.

Harrod's, Ltd., a toy store in London, logo.

The Good News Bearer, the CHOC Family Newsletter.

Behr Manning sandpaper.

108

Bear Brand pots and kettles, an Australian company, adopted a Koala theme for their trademark in 1947.

3 Koalas is the trademark of Lewis Ornstein's Sound Records, an Australian music firm, circa 1958.

OK, a Japanese department store, logo.

Logo for a Japanese women's magazine, Shufu No Fomo.

Koala brand soft drink from Australia.

TraveLodge logo.

Herman Survivor's®, a water-proof shoe.

Circa 1883 logo for Missouri Bear Brand, a waterproof clothing produced by a St. Louis, Missouri, company Jammopoulis, Co.

Zerolene trademark.

Pettijohn's Breakfast Food logo.

Symbols used by the city of Bern, Germany.

Jack Nicklaus Golden Bear Sportswear logo.

Symbol of Barrägen, a Swedish pharmaceutical/chemical company. Barrägen has used the bear grinding with mortise and pestle for 100 years. Their factory near Stockholm is located near a zoo begun by company founder Johan Wilhelm Holmström. Holmström considered bears a symbol of power and strength. The symbol is seldom used today except on the lids of Bear Glue jars and in relief on Barrägen soap.

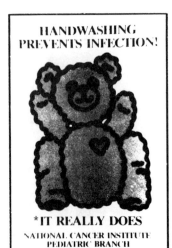

110

"BEAR In Mind OUR TRADE MARK.

PETTIJOHN'S BREAKFAST FOOD

HERE'S HOW

SET ANIMAL ON CUP LIKE THIS

FOLD ON THIS LINE

DIRECTIONS

Save your ice cream cup and wash out clean. Cut out animal carefully on the outline including the circle around these directions. Fold on the dotted line. Set round base of animal in closed end of cup when turned up-side-down. See picture of bear on cup.

CUT ON THE OUTSIDE OF THIS LINE

© 1939
PATENT APPLIED FOR

From the cover, a Dixie cup cut-out, circa 1939.

A 1984 Chinese poster promoting family planning.

一对夫妻一个孩

A 1988 Pennsylvania travel advertisement.

A 1981 Transway International Corporation advertisement for their network of transportation and distribution companies.

Kudos Granola Snackbar "Kudos K. Bear" promotional advertisement from 1989.

Brochure for new parents.

Alaska travel advertisement.

Choco Stands for Sweetness...
But Not Chocolate

Choco, the bear mascot/logo for Children's Hospital of Orange County was designed by Walt Disney Productions for the October 5, 1964, opening of the renowned institution.

Walt Disney himself expressed an interest in contributing something to the new children's hospital, since it was located in the vicinity of Disneyland. An astute board member noted that the hospital was in need of a logo, and Choco was born with a "hurt" left arm and Mickey Mouse® ears.

Choco is used on wall murals, on the inlaid lobby tile floor, and on all hospital correspondence and literature.

A hospital employee, Yvonne Nenadal, wrote *The Story of Choco Bear*, telling of a playful cub who falls out of a tree and goes to Children's Hospital for help. As the story goes: "Once inside, he was amazed at how friendly everyone was. The nurses and doctors took him to a special room where they cleaned off his cuts and bruises and wrapped his arm in soft white bandages. It was decided that he should spend the night to make sure that his arm was really okay. Choco thought this was a fine idea, since the hospital seemed like a rather fun place to be... He decided he would become a special friend of the hospital. And so he became a very busy bear, indeed, helping the children who came to the hospital in any way he could."

The 165 bed facility, a not-for-profit pediatric center, offers a wide range of medical services to over 40,000 patients annually.

READY TEDDY GO!

Teddy bears and under 5's travel free on British Rail

Advertisement for British Railways.

Family Railcard from British Railways.

114

Teddy Bear Hole-in-One

Jack Nicklaus Sportswear is a new example of a firm using a bear symbol. Nicklaus, the legendary professional golfer, has long been nicknamed the Golden Bear, because of his blond hair and large build. Now he is trying to make another winning score, this time off the course, by replacing the ubiquitous Izod alligator with a golden bear on his line of shirts, sweaters and swimsuits. His advertisements play up the bear theme to the maximum. And what could suit today's male image better...strong but gentle...than the bear?!

Jack Nicklaus Golden Bear sportswear advertisement.

1930s Spring Maid brand beans with teddy bears decorating the bowl.

Teddy bears used for "Bear Aid," a late 1980s campaign to raise funds for needy children. Bears designed by Ted Menton.

PP&L, Pennsylvania Power & Light Company, advertisement for heat pump usage in 1989.

Bear Paw ice scraper.

Dentyne gum promotional card to send a teddy bear hug to a friend.

Kodiak chewing tobacco logo.

Hershey's Panda Bar ice cream bar.

Below: *Little Rhine Bear Liebfraumilch wine, a product of Germany.*

118

1882 advertisement for French whalebone corsets. Drawing by T. Levigne.

One More for the Road

Another travel-related bear is Oliktok, a polar bear cub who has been the symbol for TravAlaska Tours for over ten years. In 1985, he was on the cover of the company's main brochure. According to Charles King, a former "bear baby sitter" for the Arctic Aeromedical Lab at Ladd Air Force Base in Alaska, in early 1959, the Fish and Wildlife Department shipped an orphaned polar bear cub to the lab from Point Oliktok.

The cub was named Oliktok, although a later bath revealed him to be a her (k is a male ending, a is a female ending in the Eskimo language).

Shortly after the cub's arrival, King met Jo Crumrine, a wildlife artist, who had come to sketch the bear. "Jo would always have some tidbit for the cub and the little bear would sit and pose for her while she sketched. Dr. Hock (in charge of the lab) said she could come and go pretty much as she pleased. This was more than he allowed any field grade officer to do, for he did not take lightly to anyone disturbing the animals. The portrait TravAlaska has of the cub is exactly as it patiently sat while Jo talked sweet nothings and fed it scraps of cooked roast beef. Even pictures my wife took of the bear at the time Jo was sketching do not catch the actual expression on the cub's face as does her portrait. Those eyes will follow you across a room as you go from one side to another," said King.

In late 1959, Senator Gruening of Alaska sent Oliktok as a gift to the boys and girls of Florida. According to King, the Senator had many photographs taken of himself with the cub, with King always just out of the camera's view, standing by in case "Oliktok decided that maybe the good senator might be a tasty morsel." However, the friendly cub was always well-behaved.

TravAlaska lost track of the bear after he went south, but his portrait hangs in the firm's executive offices, and a stylized white-on-blue polar bear is the company's symbol.

Happy Bear

Bear Automotive Service Equipment Company, headquartered in Milwaukee, Wisconsin, was founded in 1917 by brothers Will and Henry Dammann. The Bear logo, as it still appears today, was first seen in the early 1920s. It has never been reproduced as a model or stuffed toy, but does appear as a costumed character called "Happy Bear" who makes regular appearances at national trade shows, representing Bear Co. A recent addition to the Bear line of equipment is promotional clothing: caps, jackets and uniform patches, made by K-Products, Inc. of Orange City, Iowa. Information, photographs and graphics courtesy of Bear Automotive.

TravAlaska brochure cover featuring a polar bear cub, Oliktok, sketched by Josephine Crumrine.

Mover's Advantage sm

The complete home moving guide & planning kit

Ryder moving vans and trucks pamphlet cover.

From the cover, an advertisement for Roblee Shoes for Men, from Life *magazine, September 28, 1942.*

How the Bear Became a Teddy

This *Washington Post* premium calendar was offered in 1906. The calendar is the original work of Clifford Berryman, famous among bear lovers for his Berryman Bear, the subject of this calendar. The Berryman Bear first appeared in the now celebrated "Drawing the Line in Mississippi" cartoon which depicts President Teddy Roosevelt refusing to shoot a bear cub tethered to a tree, an incident that occurred November 10, 1902 in Smedes, Mississippi. The cartoon was a boon for the popularity of the stuffed bear, known forever after as "teddy bear."

The Washington Post.

Calendar

1907

April

1907					1907	
SUN	MON	TUE	WED	THU	FRI	SAT
	1	2	3	4	5	6
7	8	9	10	11	12	13
14	15	16	17	18	19	20
21	22	23	24	25	26	27
28	29	30				

May

1907					1907	
SUN	MON	TUE	WED	THU	FRI	SAT
			1	2	3	4
5	6	7	8	9	10	11
12	13	14	15	16	17	18
19	20	21	22	23	24	25
26	27	28	29	30	31	

June

1907					1907	
SUN	MON	TUE	WED	THU	FRI	SAT
						1
2	3	4	5	6	7	8
9	10	11	12	13	14	15
16	17	18	19	20	21	22
23	24	25	26	27	28	29
30						

THE ONE THAT GOT AWAY!

C K Berryman

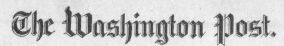

The Washington Post.

Calendar

1907

July

1907					1907	
SUN	MON	TUE	WED	THU	FRI	SAT
	1	2	3	4	5	6
7	8	9	10	11	12	13
14	15	16	17	18	19	20
21	22	23	24	25	26	27
28	29	30	31			

August

1907					1907	
SUN	MON	TUE	WED	THU	FRI	SAT
				1	2	3
4	5	6	7	8	9	10
11	12	13	14	15	16	17
18	19	20	21	22	23	24
25	26	27	28	29	30	31

September

1907					1907	
SUN	MON	TUE	WED	THU	FRI	SAT
1	2	3	4	5	6	7
8	9	10	11	12	13	14
15	16	17	18	19	20	21
22	23	24	25	26	27	28
29	30					

The Washington Post.
Calendar
1907

October
1907   **1907**

SUN	MON	TUE	WED	THU	FRI	SAT
		1	2	3	4	5
6	7	8	9	10	11	12
13	14	15	16	17	18	19
20	21	22	23	24	25	26
27	28	29	30	31		

November
1907   **1907**

SUN	MON	TUE	WED	THU	FRI	SAT
					1	2
3	4	5	6	7	8	9
10	11	12	13	14	15	16
17	18	19	20	21	22	23
24	25	26	27	28	29	30

December
1907   **1907**

SUN	MON	TUE	WED	THU	FRI	SAT
1	2	3	4	5	6	7
8	9	10	11	12	13	14
15	16	17	18	19	20	21
22	23	24	25	26	27	28
29	30	31				

About the Author

Marty Crisp, a staff reporter for the Lancaster, Pennsylvania, *Sunday News*, has a bear collection numbering well over 1000 and has written articles for such collector's magazines as **Teddy Bear and friends**®, *The Teddy Bear Review* and *Doll Stars*.

Also a registered nurse, Marty freelances for a wide variety of magazines ranging from *Family Circle* to *Nursing Life* to *Highlights for Children*. For several years she had been researching the histories of advertising bears, and says, to the best of her memory, she has never met a bear she did not like.

In 1987, her 1st romance novel, "The Stormy Heart" was published by Avalon.

PHOTO: *The author, Marty Crisp, with friend, in 1948.*

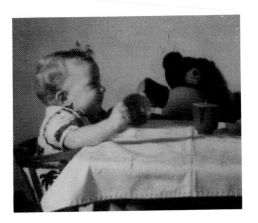

About the Photographer

George Crisp, CPA, Vice President and Treasurer for Pennrock Financial Securities Corp., has been a freelance photographer for Lancaster Newspapers' *Extra* weekly supplement and tries to keep count of the teddies in the Crisp household. Accustomed to living with teddy bears as well as four dogs and four children, George enjoys photography but will not say how he feels about the rest of it.

PHOTO: *The photographer, George B. Crisp, with friend, in 1948.*